73 950

7/12
Gibson, | ISLAND CAMERA | 942.87.

HERTFORDSHIRE LIBRARY SERVICE

This book is due for return on or before the date shown. You may extend its loan by bringing the book to the library or, once only, by post or telephone, quoting the date of return, the letter and number on gid data card, if applicable and

Please renew/return this item by the last date shown.

So that your telephone call is charged at local rate, please call the numbers as set out below:

From Area codes 01923 or 0208:	From the rest of Herts:
Renewals: 01923 471373	01438 737373
Enquiries: 01923 471333	01438 737333
Minicom: 01923 471599	01438 737599

L32b

DAMSON
8-3-88

1 2 MAR 1989

18 DEC 1995

2 0 OCT 2009

-9 JAN 1996

10 MAR 1997

1 - NUV 2002

L 33

ISLAND CAMERA

GIRLHOOD · ARANMORE

ISLAND CAMERA

The Isles of Scilly
in the photography of the Gibson family

JOHN ARLOTT
in collaboration with
REX COWAN
and
FRANK GIBSON

DAVID & CHARLES
NEWTON ABBOT

© 1972 John Arlott, Rex Cowan and
Frank Gibson
This edition published in 1972
by David & Charles (Publishers) Limited

Set in 12 on 13pt Bembo
by C. E. Dawkins (Typesetters) Limited
London SE1 and printed in Great Britain
by The Pitman Press Bath
for David & Charles (Publishers) Limited
South Devon House Newton Abbot Devon

CONTENTS

ILLUSTRATIONS

THE GIBSON FAMILY

This is a unique book because it is the product of unique circumstances. It is a pictorial history, recorded with the unarguable—or almost unarguable—precision of the camera, of over a hundred years of a single place, by the members of a single family. It is virtually impossible that such a coincidence of limitation of setting, unbroken succession of practitioners, continuity and breadth of theme, preservation and quality of results can have occurred anywhere else since the inception of photography.

For over a hundred years the Gibson family—five men in four generations—have been taking photographs in the Isles of Scilly. Their work is not duplicated there because, for most of the time, the area could not support even one professional photographer. So they undertook not only the portrait, but the press, landscape and archival work for one of the less well-known parts of Britain (and still for many years had to balance their economy by working in Penzance as well).

Of these five men, one was something of an originator; one both a creative photographer and a remarkable person; three efficient craftsmen; and all characters of strength and individuality.

The impact of the Gibsons, through tradition, island reminiscence, personal contacts and the quality of their work, changed the character and purpose of this book. It was first planned as a collection of views of Scilly. The extent and variety of the early Gibson pictures suggested a series showing the changes in the islands during the last century. Finally it

became apparent that any book of photographs about Scilly would be dominated in personality as well as weight of material by the Gibsons. Rex Cowan, who had first envisaged an illustrated book on Scilly, accepted and assisted the change of course; James and Francis (domestically and professionally Frank) Gibson, from long memories, filled in details which could never otherwise have been discovered; Frank made his albums and copyright available, and provided sharpened, extended or enlarged prints with kind promptness. Meanwhile, what had begun as a casual interest developed into absorption, enthusiasm, and a book on a highly unlikely subject—an unbroken century of professional photography of one place by one family.

John Gibson (1827-1920) began it; he was followed by his two sons, Alexander Gendall, and Herbert John Gibson; Alexander's son, James, continued it and was succeeded by one of his two sons, Francis Edward, the present incumbent of the family business.

So the 'tree' of photographers is:

John Gibson (1827-1920)

Alexander Gendall Gibson (1857-1944)   Herbert John Gibson (1861-1937)

James Gibson (1901-   )

Francis Edward Gibson (1929-   )

9

There is an unauthenticated report by an American historian, George F. Lyle, that in the eighteenth century an intending emigrant named Gibson was so seasick that, unable to continue the journey to America, he was put off at St Martin's where, it was claimed, a descendant of his, Wilfred Christopher, was living in the nineteenth century. The story is preserved, if not accepted, by the family.

The Gibsons are Scillonians of almost three hundred years' certain standing. From time to time economic necessity drove them, like many of their fellow islanders, to earn a living elsewhere: but with a tenacious loyalty they have always contrived to return. They came from St Martin's, the most easterly of the populated islands whose people—many of whom were red-headed—are by tradition the most insular of all in Scilly.

The parish registers of St Martin's record three eighteenth-century John Gibsons; one lived from roughly 1698 to 1765; another married Sarah Stephens in 1755; a third married Jane Ashford in 1783, and three years later their son, James, was born. He is recorded as marrying Catherine — or Caroline — a St Martin's girl of the well-known Scillonian family of Nance, in 1811.

Life was not easy: the islands have rarely provided more than an adequate living—often far less—for the working people. During and immediately after the Napoleonic Wars there was acute distress among the largely peasant population of Scilly. Much of the land was so savagely windswept that the crops from the inconveniently parcelled farms were meagre (the windbreak hedges that protect the modern flower fields lay well in the future); the kelp industry—burning seaweed for use in making glass—and soap—had died out; so had flax-growing and the salting of fish. Scilly salt ling once had a high reputation; but when the duty drove the price of salt to sixpence a pound it became uneconomic. Shipbuilding on the beaches of St Mary's was only beginning to grow, and the absentee Duke of Leeds had not yet been succeeded as Lord Proprietor by Augustus Smith the autocratic, reforming creator of a stable Scilly. So, after some bad harvests, the ordinary islanders' hopes of elevation even to subsistence level lay in plundering the ships frequently wrecked in those perilous waters. Even smuggling, for long regarded as a normal part of island life rather than a breach of the law, had been reduced by the introduction of a newly effective preventive system employing a locally based cutter. The formerly extensive pilotage had been reduced by regionalisation, and what remained went to St Agnes. So there was little left for the young men of Scilly except to follow their seafaring tradition, either as fishermen, which gave a bare living, or in the merchantmen out of West Country ports. This early James Gibson became a seaman but after a few years he joined the coastguard service and was posted to Aranmore—the largest island of the Aran group in Galway Bay.

There his child, another John, was born in 1827 and went to sea at the age of twelve, a year before his father—unusually short-lived for a Gibson—died at the age of 55. John and his mother returned to Scilly, and settled in St Mary's, where the widow and her son earned a scanty living from a general store in Silver Street, Hugh Town. Nicknames prevail in Scilly. On one occasion they were written into an official return as the only means of distinguishing between the members of the Jenkins, Nicholls, Pender and Ellis families who peopled Tresco. From his days at the shop, and the sale of some meat, John Gibson was given—and has retained in local memory down to the present—the nickname 'Johnny Prime'. To balance the family economy he was forced to leave his mother keeping the shop while he went back to sea.

In 1855 he married Sarah Gendall of St Mary's but soon afterwards they found it too difficult to make ends meet on St Mary's. John Gibson could find work there, but it was so poorly paid that he decided to settle in Penzance. Still he had to go to sea; and according to the account passed down through the family by word of mouth—which, wherever it can be checked is strikingly accurate—he bought a camera 'abroad'. He learnt to use it in one of the then rare establishments which taught photography and, at intervals between voyages during the early 1860s, he began to take portraits in a studio in Penzance.

This was an extremely early stage in the development of photography. Daguerre and Fox-Talbot only published their discoveries—different infant versions of the process—in 1839. The camera remained bulky, and developing both complicated and difficult, far past 1850. The taking of a photograph was an extremely uncertain process when John Gibson began to practise it. He started a little before the first appreciable English portrait photographer, Julia Margaret Cameron, whose son gave her a camera as a present in 1865. She later recalled having 'destroyed a hundred negatives before I achieved one good result'. The young sailor could not afford such an expensive degree of failure. Unlikely as it may seem, the boy who received only the smattering of cottage education doled out in Aran before he was twelve was, by his middle thirties, making a sufficiently good living—on a competitive basis—as one of the few practitioners of the newly fashionable art in his area, to give up going to sea. Now, when

he was at last established on the mainland, the tug of Scilly—with whom the Gibsons of the last hundred years have had a strange love-hate relationship—asserted itself; and in about 1866 he returned to St Mary's. The earliest surviving Gibson photograph that can be dated beyond doubt is of the ships in St Mary's Bay (plate 76) taking shelter early in the Franco-Prussian War, during the summer of 1870. Others may well be earlier.

By this time John Gibson had a studio shed in his back garden and was assisted by his elder son, Alexander Gendall Gibson, who was to become the outstanding photographer and most striking personality in the family; and for many years one of the most remarkable characters in Scilly. The family tradition is strong and unquestioned that as a small child he stood on a chair to focus the camera for his father. Like many who grow up in a household where one particular and unusual skill is practised with enthusiasm, he absorbed effortlessly what other people needed to study and contrive. He had little of the advantage his younger brother, Herbert, enjoyed of the admirable nineteenth-century educational system of Scilly. It was introduced and provided by the Lord Proprietor of the islands, Augustus Smith, who made it compulsory—almost thirty years before it became so in England—by dint of charging the parents a penny a week for each child who attended school, and twopence for each one who did not.

Alexander Gibson, however, was of the Victorian type of self-educated man, who esteemed knowledge for its own sake and had a wide range of interests. He was a voracious reader and so absorbed in archaeology, architecture and folk history, that his grandson had no doubt that he put those subjects before his business. He took a vast number of photographs of ruins, prehistoric remains, fossils, barrows, crosses, forts and artifacts, not only in Scilly but all over Cornwall, and presented them to the County Museum in Truro.

There is no doubt that, from about 1871, when he was fourteen, Alexander's technical capacity and strength of will were such that he was an influential member of his father's business; and his method is evident in most of the important photographs that remain from that period.

He had an intuitive sense of pictorial form and an ingrained realisation that a photograph of almost any inanimate object or a scene was given an added dimension by the introduction of people. If necessary he would focus the camera, take up position in the view himself (as in plate 112) while someone else released the catch, or he himself triggered it by some improvised form of remote control. His predilection for groupings, and habit of arranging people, which everyone who knew him (or his work) recalls with amusement, was never monotonous. He was too sensitive to subject for that; but he was a perfectionist to a point some of his family regarded as fussiness. Notice his different handling of the two almost identical themes of the flower farmers and their workers in plates 53 and 54, where the treatment echoes the characters of the people. He had an instinctive feeling for the moment to take his photograph, as in plate 90 where he must have recognised in an instant the human flavour imparted by the little girl who is 'lost'.

He had no objection to improving on nature—especially in respect of adding clouds to an uninteresting sky—with a few touches of photo paint; and his sails on the Buzza windmill (plate 96) and the cross of shells on Sir Clowdisley Shovell's 'grave' (plate 115)

were for him part of a creative act—or justifiable historic reconstruction. He was to turn an appreciable portion of his house in Church Street, Hugh Town, into a private museum full of his discoveries: his advertisements invited visitors to come to see it—and many of its contents form a substantial proportion of the exhibits in the present Scilly Islands museum on St Mary's. He observed, and recorded in a series of characteristic pictures, the growth of the flower industry which, after the collapse of the early potato farming, sustained the economy of the islands until the development of the tourist trade came to reinforce it.

Tall, trimly built and fastidious about his appearance, Alexander Gibson wore his hair to his shoulders, affected a black velvet cap and is remembered in Scilly now as an old man with a long white beard. He was quick of temper as well as mind; and he did not suffer fools gladly. Although he was an affectionate husband and his wife—a Tresco Jenkins—physically a big woman, she was overwhelmed by the weight of his character. He could not tolerate boredom and, fortunately for him, his nature rarely led him into it.

He was at least a competent water-colour painter, who wrote the 'official' guide to Scilly, called The Visitor's Companion in Sunny Lyonnesse which ran to several editions over more than twenty years. Enthusiastic, full of illuminating references to island life and history, it is literary in tone; it not only contains quotations from poets as widely different as Tennyson, Burns, Hood, Wordsworth, Longfellow, a Scillonian lady—Miss M. Davis—and, undoubtedly, the author himself—but also, less expectedly in such a context, from Francis Bacon, Professor T. H. Huxley, Mark Twain and Lord Levershulme.

An agnostic at a period and in a place

where that was a difficult position to maintain, and politically conscious, he spoke his mind—an agent of the Duchy of Cornwall named Jefferies once referred to him as 'that chap with a voice like a chacking gull'—but not offensively. People of this outlook and disposition were, to set it at its least, not common nor, outside the small number of the privileged, likely to be accepted in nineteenth-century Scilly, and it is surprising that Alexander Gibson's independence did not lead him into conflict with authority. Perhaps he was regarded as an eccentric; or that constant visits to his mainland shop—in Market Jew Street, Penzance—afforded a safety valve; for in adult life he spent only the summer period in St Mary's.

All this, however, lay far in the future in 1870 when John Gibson worked from a shed-studio in his back garden with his thirteen-year-old son as his assistant, and a group of Scillonians formed a telegraph company to link St Mary's with the mainland. With the laying of the cable Scilly became for the first time truly accessible in 'outside world' terms, and John Gibson was engaged as the local newspaper correspondent. Five years afterwards the German passenger steamer *Schiller*, out of New York for Hamburg, was wrecked on the Retarrier Ledges, east of the Bishop Rock light, and 311 people—all but forty-three of her passengers and crew—were lost. It was the Gibsons' story. John gathered such facts as he could; it was all extremely confused; the ship had passed inside the Bishop light in fog; her distress rockets were mistaken for the customary signals of arrival; and no rescue attempt was made for nine hours by which time she was a complete wreck. Alexander manned the cable office and transmitted his father's copy; his hand is clearly apparent, too, in the sequence of

Schiller photographs (plates 34 to 36).

After the *James Armstrong*, the earliest surviving photograph known certainly to have been taken by Alexander is of the Russian steamer *Aksai*, wrecked on White Island to the north of St Martin's in November 1875. It was no simple matter to obtain such a picture at that time. In a day of gigs for the fortunate or, more probably, simply a rowing boat, the sea passage was hard work when it was not also hazardous. Once on the island, the camera was a considerable load. In his younger days, Alexander Gibson, walking across country with his equipment slung from his shoulders, was a familiar sight in Scilly. The 12in × 10in field camera with all its paraphernalia—a developing tent, a battery of three or four lenses and plates—together weighed substantially over thirty pounds. There had to be different lenses for different plates, for no enlargements were possible. Contact prints demanded a fresh negative for each size of print. Daylight printing, before the advent of electricity, was done in a room with a north-facing window and plates were developed 'by inspection'—examined at varying stages—and might be saved by chemicals or the bleacher (ferro cyanide). The 'field' photographer often carried a developing tent with him. The wet plates were usually made up before he set out; then, as soon as the photograph was taken, he either developed it in the tent at once; or, as Alexander did in the case of the wreck of the *Aksai* (plate 30), wrapped moist rags round the slide to keep the plate wet until it could be developed.

The worthwhile financial return from the Gibsons' wreck pictures derived from their use as evidence for ship-owners making insurance or legal claims, or for crew members as souvenirs. Except in cases of major disasters like the wreck of the *Schiller*, the press was a minor economic interest; and it was not until after 1900 that the Gibsons began to issue postcards, in which their series of wrecks in the Scilly area have always attracted profitable interest.

Despite his intensity in the pursuit of his interests, Alexander Gibson was both humorous and flexible. This is apparent in his his sequence of postcards, 'A Holiday Trip' (plates 46 to 51), extremely popular in their day and still diverting, showing a group of day-trippers to Scilly in progressive stages of seasickness. The photographs are not only revealing and wryly sad; but only an extremely sea-legged, artful and efficient photographer could have taken them—especially with the equipment of 1902. He relished, too, and recounted in his *Guide*, the story of the honeymoon couple walking by the sea in Scilly when the husband, moved by the splendour of the scene to poetic emotion declaimed, 'Roll on, thou deep and mighty ocean, roll'—and his wife, in ecstasy burst out 'O, look, George, it's doing it!'

Herbert, by six years to the month the younger brother, worked as amicably with the idiosyncratic Alexander as could be expected—perhaps more—for fifty years. Alexander had the ideas, made most of the policy decisions—even if over the head of his father as well as his brother—and often wandered off in pusuit of his own hobbies. Herbert, a stockily built, quiet man, was the worker of the partnership, a competent photographer and sound in the everyday matters of business. His particular interest lay in the photographing of shipwrecks and, long after Alexander lost his enthusiasm for such treks, Herbert would set off, carrying a half plate camera, across country, scrambling down cliffs or over rocks to a vessel holed or stranded on some inaccessible stretch of coast

and work from hand to get his pictures. He respected his brother's different aptitudes; while, although the *Guide* was obviously Alexander's work to the last letter, the 'Authors' are named as Alexander G. Gibson and Herbert J. Gibson.

Meanwhile, their father, John, had settled in at Clarence House in Church Street, Hugh Town. At the beginning of this century he allowed the business gradually to pass to his sons who bought him out in 1910 and John, first and most determined of the Gibson photographers, retired to the village of St Buryan, near Penzance, where he died ten years later. Alexander's son, James, was taken into the business as soon as he left school in 1916.

The brothers maintained the dual-based business: holidaymakers and day-trippers justified their active presence in Scilly during the summer months; but they both wintered in Penzance and all their processing was done there until 1925. In that year they effectively parted when Alexander and his family went to live in Scilly and Herbert stayed on in Penzance. They legally dissolved their association in 1930; and Alexander remained the senior member of the business.

By 1934 he was rising seventy, still quick of wit and even hastier of temper, retaining many interests outside photography. His son James was now a married man with children and, after eighteen years as a junior, he wanted his independence. The business no longer satisfied Alexander who spent more and more time on the mainland—but he could neither bring himself to pass it over to his son, nor to pay him an adequate wage for running it. James could be as fiery as his father and eventually, after yet another quarrel, they parted—only for Alexander to open up an opposition studio in St Mary's.

Such a situation could not continue.

Crucially there was not room for two photographers in Scilly; secondly, Alexander was too old to conduct a one-man business efficiently even if he had retained enthusiasm for it—as he had not. Herbert came over to Scilly; but he and James could not work together and he died in 1937, when Alexander, after three bitter years in Hugh Town—which always cribbed him—went back to Cornwall, and eventually agreed to sell all he had retained of the business to James. A sum was agreed, and conditions involving all the plates of shipwrecks passing to James. Alexander delivered them all—unpacked—to Ferris the Penzance carrier; they were put straight on to the 'old' *Scillonian* with no protection, made the crossing to St Mary's and arrived completely intact. That transaction complete, Alexander threw all the other plates of Scilly subjects in his possession down a tin mine. Fortunately, much of his work still remained in the Hugh Town studio; this book would be much the poorer if it had not. That dramatically wasteful gesture made, he went to settle in Oswestry where, more than a dozen years later, in his eighties, he wrote a guide book on the local parish church. He died in 1944 at the age of eighty-seven.

A few years ago, after Frank had broadcast a talk about his grandfather, a woman in North Wales wrote to tell him she had an album of Alexander's photographs. She had bought them in a jumble sale, attracted by their quality but unaware of their history. The circumstantial evidence that they were Alexander Gibson's work on non-Scillonian themes was not to be doubted. Frank wrote back asking if he might see them but received no reply. Have they, by now, passed into another jumble sale?

James, decisive, active, a conscientious photographer who took business seriously, had struggled for thirty years to control the Gibson business and, having taken hold on it, he was reluctant to relinquish it. So the situation of the previous generation was repeated. As soon as his elder son, Frank, had left school, in 1946, he went into the family business to work for his father. He, in his turn, married, had a family and wanted the status of a family man. After such disagreement as is always to be expected between father and son in long-lived families where succession is the only success, James sold out to Frank in 1958.

Frank Gibson has extended the scope of the Gibson business. Constantly concerned to carry out the varying types of work demanded of a professional photographer, he has a craftsman's appreciation of his equipment and has retained the family enthusiasm for the art. Photography, though, is no longer economically enough but he does not neglect that branch and, a Gibson at heart, in addition to the bread-and-butter sale of books and fancy goods, he makes many photographs for the satisfaction of maintaining his family's pictorial history of Scilly in the time of the camera.

The fifth — fourth-generation — Gibson photographer of Scilly has three daughters and no son; his brother, a bank employee, has three sons not yet old enough to show any formative desire to become photographers. Thus it must be possible that this remarkable succession will end with its present inheritor. Even if that should be so, it will leave behind a rare, tangible, diverting and valuable pictorial record of its life and times in the Isles of Scilly. This has been a durable and long-working family. John Gibson lived for 94 years, 46 of them as a photographer; Alexander to 87, 66 in the business, undoubtedly taking pictures for longer than that; Herbert died at 75 after nearly 60 years in the family concern; James, still a lively 71, carried on for 42 years;

Frank, 42 after 26 years of business, should have long to go. So, between the five of them, they have been responsible for 240 professional photography-years on the Isles of Scilly, which—even without those unguessable and unique plates that Alexander cast down the tin mine—have produced a range of pictures of people, events, scenes and objects which form simultaneously a frozen, a human and a gossipy history of a century of life in the Isles of Scilly; a picture book; an island story; and the autobiography of a family.

SCILLONIANS

The people of Scilly are, perhaps surprisingly, neither so distinctive nor so identifiable as might be expected of those who live in—by British standards—relative remoteness. In the New Forest, rural Wiltshire, Dorset, the Forest of Dean, pockets of the Black Country, east Suffolk, the Highlands and islands of Scotland and many parts of Wales, the population groups are more sharply defined. Scilly contains an appreciably smaller proportion of long-established families.

The basic reason for this relative lack of local character is that the population in general did not endure. Until the last hundred years or less it was not a comfortable place for any but the privileged—who were few, indeed—to live. Although Scilly was inhabited at least three thousand years ago, it is doubtful if any of the present names existed in the islands before the mid-seventeenth century. The long-established families, most of them descended from the Godolphins or their employees, have infallibly had two characteristics in common—durability and determination—reflected in willingness to turn their hands to plough or tiller in season to make a living.

Those who do not know Scilly may think of it as a natural flower garden; and early and splendid flowers do grow there—but mostly under glass or protected by feet-thick hedges from the scouring winds; and even in high summer the fogs can be so thick as to bring a great ship blundering to destruction on the thicket of ledges and rocks in its waters.

The Romans banished heretics to Scilly; for centuries the islands were pillaged by sea raiders from all over Europe. In the sixteenth century Leland wrote 'few men be glad to inhabit these islettes'; and Camden, with longer-lived significance, 'The inhabitants are all newcomers but remains show much previous habitation'. For many years absentee landlords allowed the economy, the land and the people to fall behind mainland progress into poverty. Few of the families that have survived can have done so without many an urge to leave, quelled only by the occupation of land, or even a cottage.

Traditionally each island had distinctive differences of physique and character, separate nicknames; and fierce loyalties were bred out of competition—most of it over their native waters. Those differences have increasingly disappeared as the men of Scilly travelled, more often and more easily, not only from island to island, but all over the world. In earlier centuries, even though many people left, there was undoubtedly a dangerous degree of inbreeding in Scilly, especially on the 'off' islands. It did not prove irretrievably damaging because sailors from and to the islands, imported estate employees, naval deserters, fishermen, garrison troops and even people rescued from shipwrecks introduced fresh strains; but the margin of safety was often narrow. In more recent years the danger has been completely removed; new families from the mainland—even war-time land girls returning to marry island men—and the constantly changing holiday and hotel trade communities, have made St Mary's, in particular, quite cosmopolitan by former standards. Yet there remains a distinguishable gap between the old and the new families, even if no clear and definable Scillonian character.

All new settlers in Scilly, especially those of recent years, tend to pick up background and traditions quickly and to associate themselves with the community. The enduring distinction is essentially that between those whose ancestors weathered the acute difficulties and hardships which existed until at least the middle of the last century, and those who came later when the prospect was so much more attractive. If St Mary's has become relatively non-insular, there are still important old families—probably about forty—in the islands, the greater proportion on the 'off' islands, though even they have become increasingly part of a general community.

The Gibsons, Scillonians themselves, have shown in their work—probably instinctively—an ability to detect and record the unobvious, but essential, Scillonian quality.

1   Jacob Deason of St Agnes by Alexander Gibson

Jacob Deason came of a long-established St Agnes seafaring family. This photograph, taken about 1895, was used for a postcard which the Gibsons sold well until the 1930s with the title 'An Old Smuggler'. Smuggling was so much part of life in the Isles that no old Scillonian would have resented the label; and in this instance it was probably true. The photographer has made good the tilt of the porch floor with a plank and a chopper.

2 Captain Tiddy by Herbert Gibson

Samuel Tiddy, the last of the original, unbroken line of Scillonian-born masters in the St Mary's-Penzance service, died on the bridge of the steamship *Lyonesse* in 1910.

3 Augustus Smith by John Gibson

Augustus Smith was not a Scillonian by birth (he came from Hertfordshire) but he re-created the islands and virtually saved them from ruin. In 1834, after many years of mismanagement by the agents of the Godolphin-Osborne family, he took up the lease of the Isles of Scilly from the Crown 'for the span of three lives'; and he himself ruled the archipelago as 'Lord Proprietor' (though in fact he was neither) for thirty-eight years. Although he was for a dozen years Liberal MP for Truro, he was a complete—and somewhat eccentric—autocrat; but a benevolent one. He fostered shipbuilding at St Mary's; built churches and schools; provided education; set up a Victorian—baronial—'Abbey' residence on Tresco, where, by vast effort and expenditure, he established a remarkable, sub-tropical 'outdoor Kew', and the harbour of New Grimsby. Ironically called 'Emperor', he lifted the islands to the brink of solvency, an operation completed when the flower industry flourished under the informed encouragement of his nephew and heir, Lieutenant T. Algernon Dorrien-Smith (nicknamed 'King' Smith). Augustus also introduced deer, rabbits of different colours, and ostriches to the islands.

4 Augustus Smith and St Agnes pilots, by John
Gibson, 1871.
Augustus Smith sits front right; on his right is—
it is believed—his agent. The remainder—by then
effectively the senior pilots of Scilly—are the
pilots based on St Agnes.

5 Mrs Mary Nance by Alexander Gibson
'Aunt' Mary Nance, of one of the oldest Scillonian
families, carding wool: astute photographic use of
natural light, c 1900.

6 Captain Jenkins by Alexander Gibson, 1930.
Captain 'Stee' Jenkins owned a coaster out of
St Mary's; both he and his son, Bert, did relief-
duty turns on the Bishop light.

7 Eric Guy by Frank Gibson.
Lobster fisherman and boatman, tying up at the
Quay at St Mary's.

8   John Tregear by John Gibson, c 1870

A long-remembered St Mary's character under Buzza Hill before any houses were built beyond the rookery in Church Street: a wet plate print.

9   Sarah Pender by Alexander Gibson.

'Little Sarah' was a remarkably small person—she is here standing at full height—and well-liked character on Bryher. Children were fascinated by the fact that she had five fingers (as well as a thumb) on each hand, and six toes on each foot. She and her mother, 'Aunt Sarah' (a name of mystic significance in Scilly) sold teas during the summer from their house, which is still there—the first on the left going up from Bryher quay to the main houses. Both Sarahs fell mortally ill at the same time in 1944, the daughter upstairs, the mother down. When Little Sarah died first, her body was passed out through the bedroom window to spare her mother the agonising realisation that she was dead. They were buried together in Bryher churchyard within a few days of each other, Little Sarah 73 years old and Aunt Sarah 98.

10   Off the end of the Quay by Frank Gibson. A modern study looking east from St Mary's Quay.

11   Three generations of an Old Town family by Alexander Gibson. A commissioned outdoor portrait of Mrs Watts junior (driving), Mrs Watts senior, and Miss Watts at the Parade in Hugh Town. Hugh Watts was one of the founders of the flower industry in Scilly.

12 The Wesleyan Methodist Parliament, 1890, by John Gibson.

The Wesleyan minister and his wardens. Their chapel, which was in Garrison Lane, is now the bottom end of the cinema. A commissioned photograph: purely Victorian with little hint of Scilly.

13 Matt Lethbridge, junior, by Frank Gibson.

Young Matt, who succeeded his father as coxswain of the St Mary's lifeboat, is making a crab pot; crab and lobster are the most profitable forms of fishing now practised in Scilly. There is a particularly good sale for lobsters to France.

14   The St Mary's branch of the Independent Order of Rechabites, by James Gibson. A group taken at Hugh Town, about 1935. The order was quite strong in Scilly in the earlier part of this century; there is a 'Rechabite Slipway' on Town Beach beside Holgates Hotel

15   The Nance family by Alexander Gibson. Jim Nance and his wife, of Bleak House, St Martin's, had seven daughters. He was disappointed that he had no sons; but the daughters worked like men on the farm; no task was too rough, dirty or strenuous for them; and their standard of efficiency was high. Alexander, a close friend of the family and a constant visitor, has 'arranged' the group both characteristically and, probably, with a degree of subtle mischief.

16   The Mumford Family by Alexander Gibson. John Mumford, of Newford, St Mary's with his wife, son and two daughters; taken in the Hugh Town studio.

SHIPS AND THE SEA

The Isles of Scilly and all the people of their history have not only been dependent upon the sea, but inextricably involved with it, its sound never long out of their ears. Even today, fog—as likely in midsummer as at any other time—can delay the steamer from the mainland, ground the helicopter, and leave the islands without papers or mail, or gales make the passage from Penzence appallingly uncomfortable.

Scillonians are a small group of people in a hugely important place. These islands are the hub of the mercantile traffic lanes, and strategically a key naval point, of the Western ocean. Their bays and channels have been alternately a haven and a graveyard for the ships of the world; and their men—and sometimes their women, too—have followed every form of sea employment. For many centuries, from Saxon times onwards, they were notorious for piracy; and in 1549 no less a person than Lord Admiral Seymour was executed for, among other offences, using Scilly as a pirate base.

They have been fishermen since the earliest days; at their most prosperous they produced pilchards—even for shipment to the Mediterranean—ling, mackerel and mullet; latterly crab and lobster, of high quality and in impressive quantity. At the other end of the scale, in days of poverty, they almost subsisted off limpets.

The nineteenth-century parson-local-historian George Woodley (the S.P.C.K. 'Minister of St Martin's and St Agnes'), described Scilly as 'a nursery for skilful pilots and hardy seamen'; and the Scilly pilots formed something of a maritime aristocracy. In the mid-nineteenth century thirty-two licensed branch pilots were living in Scilly. For incoming vessels this is the threshold of the British seas, the entrance to the English, Bristol and St George's channels, whose passages demand expert knowledge. The ships waited and the pilots of Scilly competed for their hire, racing out to them in the pilot gigs in which island crews still compete against one another in rowing races. Once aboard, a pilot might be long away; perhaps taking a ship to Glasgow, another down to Cardiff and a third back to Scotland, and so on, before he returned. Eventually all the Scillonian pilots were based on Agnes, the most westerly and convenient of the habitable islands. They enjoyed considerable respect both on the Islands and in the professional maritime circles of the world.

Shipbuilding effectively began in Scilly during the first quarter of the nineteenth century. In 1864, thirty-five wooden ships to a total tonnage of 6,148 were registered there. Yet in 1878 the last vessel came off the stocks at Town Beach and the industry came to an end, curiously enough at a time when craft of this type were still being built in a number of yards in southern and western England.

Many of the vessels were manned by Scillonians since for many years seagoing was the most rewarding livelihood available to them. They were instinctive sailors, the sea virtually their native element; traffic between the islands, even across the Town harbour, was a matter of stepping into a boat.

The sea was, too, their enemy. There is no grimmer Island saying than 'For every man of us who dies a natural death, the sea takes nine'. The loss of nineteen young men from

Samson sailing a French prize to Devonport during the Napoleonic wars, left the families of that island so short of labour that the Lord Proprietor, Augustus Smith, ordered the evacuation of the island for the second and last time. According to legend, too, in the sixteenth century, the entire population of Agnes was lost in a gale while returning from a wedding at Old Town St Mary's. There is no confirmation of the story, but such traditions usually have a substratum of truth and, in any event, it crystallises the emotion of a sea-tied people to the sea.

Shipwreck has always been part of life in Scilly. More vessels have gone down in those waters than in any other comparable area in the world. To the poorer section of the population this could bring otherwise unattainable wealth. The whole philosophy of seagoing peoples dictates assistance for ships in distress and, though some of the wreckers viewed it ruefully, one of the earliest of modern lighthouses was built on St Agnes in 1680; while the record of the pilot gigs, the Scilly lifeboat and even the packet boats in the saving of life at sea is vastly impressive. The contents of lost ships were a different matter, and the islanders were adept in locating, salvaging, transporting and con-

cealing them. Not a house of the older times was without its 'souvenir' of some ship wrecked among the islands.

Smuggling, too, was long regarded as a normal and defensible activity; at one period it is obvious that the landlord Godolphins themselves were involved. Islanders thought little of rowing one of the pilot gigs to France and returning by night with a load of contraband; and there was a flourishing illicit commerce with ships returning up Channel from overseas.

Modern preventive methods have changed the shape of smuggling and removed it from the pattern of life in Scilly. Similarly, more, and more efficient, lighthouses and electronic navigational aids have reduced the dangers of the rocks and ledges of Scilly. In recent times expertly planned and manned diving operations have been carried out on sites of far earlier wrecks, such as the *Association* and the *Hollandia*, located by sophisticated electronic equipment.

Meanwhile the wreck of the *Torrey Canyon* afforded a salutary reminder that the sea is never mastered. The knowledge that those who live by the sea may die by the sea is always at the back of the minds of those who exist as closely beside it as this.

17   The *Cactus*
by John Gibson.

In August 1875, this small Italian sailing ship, from Tripoli for Cardiff, ran on the Northern Rocks in fog. Local pilots floated her off, ran her ashore in the shallow channel between Samson and Bryher, and next day brought her to St Mary's quay where this photograph was taken.

18 The Mount's Bay fleet, about 1900, by Alexander Gibson. The Cornish pilchard fishermen often called at St Mary's. As strict sabbatarians they always observed Sunday at anchor, refusing to fish—and resentful of those east-coast fleets that did.

19 The Penzance fleet, by Herbert Gibson. Making to windward after pilchard, about 1900.

20　Town Beach, by John Gibson. Taken in about 1870; shipbuilding was still in progress and the Hugh Town Customs House had not yet been built.

21 Looking down the Strand, by Alexander Gibson. A brigantine is on the slip and, beyond, the local fishing boats are drawn up on the beach.

22 The *David Auterson*, by John Gibson. This picture can be dated as late as 1870; this barque, the last vessel ever built on Porthcressa, was launched in 1871; and her first voyage was a circumnavigation of the world—Cardiff, London, Sydney, Mauritius, London.

23 The *Gleaner*
by Alexander Gibson.

The *Gleaner*, a brigan-
tine, was the last ship
(excepting some fishing
smacks) ever built on
Scilly. Constructed on
a site where Holgates
Hotel now stands, she
was launched with her
masts stepped (1878).

24 The *Eri* by John Gibson. The wreck of this schooner—on White Island, St Martin's—has usually
been dated 1869 and regarded as one of the earliest Gibson photographs; but recent research suggests
that it happened in 1871. It is nevertheless quite early and represents a considerable physical achievement
for a man with the wet plates and field equipment of the time.

25 The launching of the lifeboat *Cunard* by James Gibson.

Flora Robson, who is related to the Sedgman family of St Mary's, performed the ceremony. She is shaking hands with 'old' Matt Lethbridge, the coxswain. On the left are 'Captain' Waldron Phillips and Tom Bodilly; on the right, Sam Rogers the Hugh Town blacksmith, with the hammer used to knock out the pin to launch the boat.

26 The *James Armstrong* by Alexander Gibson.

The hulk of the wrecked *James Armstrong* was towed into St Mary's before 1880 and is here being broken up on the town beach; next to it is the pilot cutter. With the 'arrangement' of bystanders, this is a typical Alexander composition; taken on a wet plate.

27 The *Minnehaha* by Alexander Gibson. In January 1874, after a disagreement between the captain and the Channel pilot, the *Minnehaha*—from Callao to Dublin—ran under full sail on to the Jolly Rocks at the southern end of St Mary's. Deeply holed, she sank almost at once. The mate and nine members of the crew climbed into the rigging and, later, off on to the rocks of the shore; the captain, the pilot and the remainder of the crew were drowned. The *Minnehaha*, fourteen months out from South America, was uninsured. Her ship's bell, brought up by a diver in 1964, is now in the museum in Hugh Town. By coincidence, thirty-six years later, another ship of the same name ran aground on Scilly Rock, but was refloated.

28   The *Earl of Lonsdale* by Alexander Gibson. In 1885 this vessel, ten miles off course and steaming at speed through fog, drove remarkably into the Smith Sound, the narrow passage between St Agnes and Annet. She became a complete wreck and broke up a few weeks later. In the foreground—admirable bonus for a photographer—is the 'Troy Town' maze of St Agnes; sometimes said to have been made by a bored lighthouse keeper, and probably several times reconstructed, its true origin is unknown.

29   The *Longships*, by James Gibson. In 1939 this Scottish-owned cargo steamer broke her back on the Seven Stones Reef, a most lethal rock formation for several centuries of shipping.

30   The *Aksai*, by Alexander Gibson. The Russian steamer *Aksai* ran on to White Island, north of St Martin's, in fog on 2 November 1875. The *Lady of the Isles*, the newly commissioned Penzance-St Mary's packet boat, took off the captain and crew, leaving the vessel to break up.
Alexander was in charge of the business in Scilly at this time, while his father was in Penzance. A note on this photo in John's hand reads: 'Alex Gibson, then about seventeen years old and alone in Scilly, went in the gig *Lloyds* to St Martin's to photograph the *Aksai*. He had to prepare two wet plates, all he could take; Russian sailors helped him across the island with his gear and he secured a distant and a near view of the wreck. He had to keep wetting cloths around the slides to keep the plates from drying. He had a rough passage back and had been away five hours, a most unusual time for wet plates, but got very good results. He got an order from the captain for forty-five copies at half a crown each and remembered to get him to sign his order.'

31 The *Earl of Arran* by Alexander Gibson. On a day trip from Penzance this paddle steamer was running late for St Mary's when a member of a local pilot boat crew—though not a qualified pilot—suggested to the captain that he could take him in by a short cut through Great English Island Neck between St Martin's and Nornour. The master, Captain Deason, allowed him to take over; almost at once the ship was holed by a rock, had to be beached on Nornour and, though everyone aboard and the cargo were saved, the ship became a complete loss and Captain Deason's licence was suspended for four months. The steamer's boiler still lies on the rocks at the south-west end of the island. (Taken on 10in. x 12in. camera.)

32 The *Pasteur* by James Gibson. A French crab fishermen's boat, the *Pasteur*, ran aground beside Hanjague Rock when the wind dropped as she was sailing out of St Mary's. Before she floated off on the next tide she made James Gibson a piece of photographic form worthy of his father.

33   The *Reginald* by Alexander Gibson. When this Plymouth trawler ran aground at Porth Hellick, the crew refused to stay aboard because she was stranded at such an acute angle. They brewed up tea and waited for her to slide down on the next full tide—as she duly did.

34 The *Schiller* lifeboat by John Gibson.

The German passenger liner *Schiller*—from New York bound for Plymouth and Hamburg—passed unknowingly inside the Bishop light in fog on the night of 7 May 1875 and struck the Retarrier ledges. Of her 354 passengers and crew, 311 were killed. Only two of her eight boats cleared the wreck; they landed at Tresco and this photograph, poignant in its implications, shows one of them on the Town Beach at Hugh Town.

35 Digging graves for the dead of the *Schiller* by Alexander Gibson.

Some of the recovered bodies were embalmed and sent to America; but the majority—147—were buried, in ceremonies spread over three days, in mass graves blasted out of the rock in Old Town churchyard.

36 Filling in the _Schiller_ graves by Alexander Gibson.

The rock was replaced on the graves after almost the entire population of St Mary's had followed the coffins—borne in pairs on donkey carts—to the interment. Memorials were erected in the churchyard to other victims whose bodies were not recovered.

37 The _Plympton_ by Alexander Gibson.

This 2,869 ton cargo steamer, on a passage to Dublin from Falmouth with grain, met heavy fog south of St Agnes on the morning of 14 August 1909, and, with her foghorn at full blast, ran on to Lethegus reef. A gig put out from St Mary's and found the vessel with her bows jammed between rocks. As soon as the fog cleared, the rescuers saw the twenty-three crew members to the safety of their lifeboats and then, in time-honoured Scillonian fashion, began to 'salvage' all they could from the wreck.

38   Alongside the *Plympton* by Alexander Gibson. The prow of the wreck is left foreground of the
photograph. Some of the crew of the *Plympton*, including the captain's wife with some pieces of china,
have loaded their baggage into a lifeboat and are about to leave the vessel. The Scillonians in the gig
are tying up to the steamer as others come out to join them.

40   The *Poleire* by Frank Gibson.

This Cypriot motor vessel, on a passage from Dublin to Gdynia, surprisingly failed to hear the Round Island lighthouse foghorn and ran aground west of Tresco in 1970. Within a few days she broke in two and sank, but local divers recovered some of the structure and contents.

39 The sinking of the *Plympton* by Alexander Gibson.

Only a few hours after she first struck, and while the salvage crew were still at work, the *Plympton* floated off the reef on a flood tide, turned turtle and went straight down in fifteen fathoms of water. Two bearers of well-known island names, Charles Mumford from St Mary's and Charles Hicks of Agnes, were drowned, while a visitor who had helped to man the gig went down, but had the luck to escape from the wheelhouse through a porthole. Eleven years later the German steamship *Hathor* sank directly on top of the *Plympton*.

41 Objects recovered from HMS *Association*, by Frank Gibson.

In 1707 the British fleet under Admiral Sir Clowdisley Shovell, returning from the Mediterranean, was driven off course by a series of gales, lost its bearings and, in darkness, drove on to the Western Rocks. The flagship, *Association*, struck Gilstone—at the extreme south-western corner of the group—and *Eagle*, *Romney* and *Firebrand* went down in the same area. By the standards of its time it was the most severe naval tragedy Britain had suffered. Two thousand officers and men were lost. The admiral was washed up at Porth Hellick at the south-west corner of St Mary's. There are conflicting and macabre reports as to what subsequently happened to him. It is certain, however, that he was buried on the foreshore near where he was found—as was always customary with shipwreck victims in Scilly, and the corpse was later disinterred and given a state funeral in Westminster Abbey. Much was recovered from these wrecks, particularly that of the *Association* by various official and unofficial searchers who found the remains and artifacts of this photograph in 1967.

42 Silver coins recovered from the *Hollandia*, by Frank Gibson.

Top L. to R. silver rider of United Provinces of Holland, 1742: Ducaton of Phillip of Spain and Netherlands, 1703.
Centre: Coin of four reales 1740, minted in Mexico City.
Bottom L. to R.: "Cob" of eight reales minted in Mexico City: coin of eight reales, Phillip V, minted in Mexico City.
The *Hollandia*, an outward bound Dutch East Indiaman, struck on the isolated Gunners—a reef due north of the Western Rocks—in 1743 and sank with all her complement of three hundred. A hundred-and-fifty-feet long and of about 700 tons, *Hollandia* was a new ship, on her maiden voyage. Part of her cargo was 129,000 silver guilders, many of which—some shown here—were recovered in diving operations during the autumn and winter of 1971.

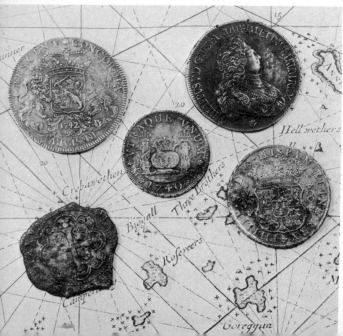

43 From the top of the Bishop by James Gibson. Winching baggage up to the lighthouse from Captain Stee's relief boat.

44 Storm breakers at Garrison by Frank Gibson. A south-westerly gale; sea breaks thunderously on this western side of St Mary's; a typical Scilly sky.

45 Calm in St Mary's Pool by Frank Gibson. Craft moored off Town Beach on a mist-still islands autumn day

A HOLIDAY TRIP

This series of six postcards devised, photographed and published by Alexander Gibson, was highly popular for some years before World War I. It has hardly been seen since then, and its wry truth may make a fresh impact on another generation: fashion changes, but the sea and seasickness remain the same.

A HOLIDAY TRIP.

No. 1.   "TROUBLE BREWING."   GIBSON, PENZANCE. COPYRIGHT

No. 2.   "A FIRST TASTE OF THE ATLANTIC."   GIBSON, PENZANCE. COPYRIGHT

No. 3.   "EFFECT OF A CROSS SEA"   GIBSON, PENZANCE. COPYRIGHT.

No. 4.   "FAR, FAR FROM LAND."   GIBSON, PENZANCE.   COPYRIGHT.

No. 5.   "LIFE BECOMES A BURDEN."   GIBSON, PENZANCE. COPYRIGHT.

No. 6.   "A GENERAL COLLAPSE."   GIBSON, PENZANCE. COPYRIGHT

THE FLOWER INDUSTRY

The flower industry lifted Scilly, narrowly but distinctly, clear of the need to depend upon Augustus Smith's subsidies. In fact it became established under his heir, Lieut T. A. Dorrien-Smith, a student of horticulture.

In such a mild climate, wild flowers had always grown freely in the sheltered parts of the islands. William Trevellick, of Rocky Hill Farm, St Mary's, a descendant of one of the Cornishmen introduced by the Godolphins to repeople St Martins in the sixteenth century, used to collect them to plant out in his garden. They flourished there and in 1881, as an experiment, he sent some of them—island tradition has it, in a hat box—to Covent Garden. By happy accident his venture coincided with the fashion for cut flowers. He received in return a cheque for £1, sufficiently strong argument, at a time when the islands' cultivation of early potatoes was failing before foreign competition, to persuade him and several other St Mary's farmers to turn their attention to flower growing.

Within a decade the islands were dispatching two hundred tons of flowers a year to the London market; in later years the figure reached a thousand tons—sixty million blooms.

The crucial factor in the success of the flower industry in Scilly lies in the fact that, since snow and severe frost are almost unknown there, they can produce crops from late November or early December until the major and most splendid blossoming in March, while it is winter on the mainland.

The original—virtually the classic—flower of the Scilly crop is the prolific yellow 'Soleil d'Or'; the 'Paper White' is another early narcissus; and 'King Alfred' and 'Fortune' are profitable daffodils. The earliest crops used to be forced under glass; subsequently by pre-heating and pre-cooling of bulbs. Nowadays the flowers are packed in bud and reach the market ready to blossom. The extension of outdoor cultivation to less sheltered parts was made possible in the shelter of thick, quick-growing floral hedges of *veronica*, *pittosporum*, *euonymous* and *escallonia* grown to break the force of the gales which often continue far into a sunny spring.

Although he never farmed, Alexander Gibson was an early enthusiast for the flower industry in Scilly; and the first organised commercial consignments of blooms were packed in his 'Lyonesse' studio.

In recent years the industry, with its small 'squares', suffered much from competition, especially from the Channel Islands; and it needed a programme of rationalisation and group marketing to restore its equilibrium. It is now again in a healthy, if not a financially dominant, position. The historian of the future will probably deduce that the flower industry kept the economy stable until the holiday trade provided a new source of income.

52 William Trevellick, by Alexander Gibson.

The 'father' of the Scillonian flower industry, top-hatted in one of his hedge-protected flower fields on Rocky Hill Farm, St Mary's. With him is E. N. V. Moyle who married Mr Trevellick's niece.

53 William Trevellick by Alexander Gibson.

In this group, taken in the glasshouse at Rocky Hill, William Trevellick is front right, his wife front left; second right, centre back and second left are the three Misses Nance—known as 'Faith', 'Hope' and 'Charity'. The blooms are 'Grand Monarques'. This was a popular postcard in its time.

54 Flower farmer and bunchers by Alexander Gibson.

George Woodcock with his wife, sons Joe and Tommy, and daughters Nelly and Mary at Lower Rocky Hill, St Mary's in the early days of the industry. A peasant setting as distinct from the patrician of the two preceding plates; and a striking contrast to the immediately previous semi-feudal grouping. George Woodcock was one of the earliest of the flower farmers, a worker rather than a director of labour.

55 Flower pickers by Alexander Gibson.
A romantic, pre-Raphaelite style composition.

56   St Martin's by Frank Gibson.
An aerial view showing the wind-break hedges of the small flower squares.

57   Taking flowers to the quay at St Martin's by Alexander Gibson.

This photograph (about 1910) was one of a series designed to illustrate the history of the Scilly flower industry. The Gibson family came from St Martin's; but Alexander's enthusiasm for visiting the island may not have stemmed entirely from family feeling. Certainly he often went there for a picture he could have procured elsewhere at cost of less time, travel, and trouble.

58 Taking flowers by gig from St Martin's, by Alexander Gibson. Taking flowers—in the wooden boxes since superseded by cardboard cartons—to the steamer at St Mary's: 1910

59 At St Martin's Quay by Frank Gibson. By comparison with the previous picture fifty years later, more flowers, more speed; cardboard cartons; powered vessel: 1960.

60 Town Quay, St Mary's by Herbert Gibson. Home-made wooden flower boxes being loaded on
to the *Lyonesse:* about 1910.

61   The Quay, Penzance, by Alexander Gibson.

Flowers from St Mary's being unloaded from the *Lyonesse* at Penzance to be taken to the railway station for the train called the 'Flower Special'.

62   Ploughing in flower bulbs, by Alexander Gibson.

The ploughman, working for 'Uncle Boss' Nance on St Martin's, has bound feathers round the chains to prevent them chafing the horse. The sandy soil, excellent for early flowers, is typical of St Martin's; church tower in the distance.

EVENTS

Scilly is impressively cool towards local events there that make national headlines. At times the reporters in the centre of Hugh Town seem almost to outnumber the visible residents; but the islanders refuse to become excited. News to them is an island matter; they are insular and would not question the fact.

Royal visits are part of the pattern of island life because every Prince of Wales since the Black Prince, as Duke of Cornwall, has been their landlord. The duchy owns all Scilly except Hugh Town, of which it sold the free-holds to the occupiers in 1949. Harold Wilson has had a house in Scilly for many years; when he became Prime Minister, that was a local matter. The *Torrey Canyon* disaster was another shipwreck; since Scilly has had more of them than any other group of islands it is less surprised by another than the rest of the world might be. Nevertheless events happen in Scilly, some of them of worldwide importance. For more than a hundred years the Gibsons have recorded them for posterity, while the Scillonians have observed them with interest rather than awe.

63   King Edward VII by Herbert Gibson. The King is being driven down Garrison on his way from Star Castle. Lieut T. A. Dorrien-Smith is sitting beside him; the coachman is John Hartley. The Royal Yacht is at anchor in the roadstead: 1902.

64   The Prince of Wales by James Gibson. The Prince, later King Edward VIII, is at Pelistry, talking to 'Tommer' Tregear who, by sheer hard work, made rough land there fit for flower farming. Mrs Tregear is on the left, Tommer's son Jack in the trilby hat, and on the right the duchy agent is signalling to James Gibson that he is only allowed to take one photograph: 1933.

65 Queen Elizabeth and the Prince of Wales by Frank Gibson.

Lieut-Commander Dorrien-Smith is beside the Queen; taken at Tresco in 1967. There are no cars on Tresco: on ceremonial occasions there, the Dorrien-Smiths travel by pony trap.

66 Harold Wilson by Frank Gibson.

In 1965 the then Prime Minister, who has a cottage on St Mary's, gave a press conference on Samson while he was spending a holiday in Scilly. He was photographed for the press and filmed for television; and answered questions on Singapore, Anglo-Russian relations, trade figures and the prospects of a Liberal-Labour coalition.

67 May Day in Hugh Town by John Gibson.

Taken about 1876 in The Parade—then the centre of the Square; this was a major annual event in St Mary's.

68 'Nickla Thies' by Alexander Gibson. This picture, taken in 1872, is one of the earliest certainly credited to Alexander Gibson; and it is characteristic of his work. The end of the harvest was always celebrated by a 'Nickla Thies' party at the 'House of the Mow' when, after a meal, dancing went on until dawn. This—obviously posed—group was taken at Trewince Farm, St Mary's. Squire Davis is in his trap at the centre of the picture. Others are his wife, daughter, baby and their nurse; the Misses Emily and Polly Tregarthen; Charles Allen, Clement Mumford, Augustus Jackson, a Customs officer named Hinks, William Escott (with his children), Stephen Bickford (in the tall hat), William Charles Bickford (holding the pony's head) and George Webber (of Old Town).

69   Gig Race by Herbert Gibson. The original purpose of the gigs was to take pilots out to vessels waiting to make the passage of the Channel. At that time there were pilots on every inhabited island and transporting them, in the gigs stationed on each island, amounted to a race, the winning of which could be of considerable value to the first pilot to reach the ship, since he might receive not simply one, but a series of engagements. The subsequent rationalisation which based all pilots of Scilly on Agnes ended that specific competition. The gigs, however, still exist and compete: from spring to autumn six of them—with, at the peak of the season, a 'guest' from the mainland—race over a course between a mark off Samson and Hugh Town Quay.

70   A Church Picnic by John Gibson. Held at Peninnis in the 1870s.

71　Auction on Town Quay (1) by James Gibson.
In 1933 some French crab fishermen were caught
fishing inside the three-mile limit and their
sentence included the confiscation of their catch
and gear which is here being auctioned by the
Customs Officer.

72　Auction on Town Quay (2) by James Gibson.
Harold Saundrey, Lloyds' agent who was also a
fish buyer for France (centre), acting as interpreter
at the auction of the French fishermen's catch—
mostly lobsters, to be seen between the pots—and
gear.

73 Edward Ward leaving Bishop Rock light by James Gibson.

The BBC commentator Edward Ward was sent to the Bishop to take part in the BBC's main feature programme on Christmas Day 1951. He duly made his contribution and was to have returned to the mainland on Boxing Day, but the weather became so severe that—to the immense interest of the national press—he was forced to spend the next three weeks on the lighthouse and even then had to be taken off by the St Mary's lifeboat.

74 *Lively Lady* by Frank Gibson.

As Alec—later Sir Alec—Rose came towards the end of his single-handed voyage round the world in 1968, he approached Scilly in thick fog and with a naval escort. He was world news: all the media were searching for him and Frank Gibson was commissioned by the BBC to find and photograph him. He set out with Alfred Jenkins—grandson of Captain "Stee"— a Scillonian who holds a master's ticket, in the *Guiding Star*, which has no modern navigational aids beyond a compass. Alfred Jenkins took them on to *Lively Lady*'s course by dead reckoning. Then he shut off his engine and listened for the foghorns of passing ships, knowing he could distinguish between the note of a naval and a merchant ship; he made his identification and this was the first photograph of the returning navigator, located eight miles south-west of the Bishop.

WAR

The position of Scilly, which once left it isolated and vulnerable and then made it an important strategic position in sea warfare, has involved it in widely different fashion in the different wars. In the fourteenth century it was raided by Welsh troops; in the Civil War, Prince Charles sheltered there before the islands surrendered to the Parliamentary army. It was defended and garrisoned against the Dutch and, later, Napoleon. With the development of flying, its situation made it a valuable base for air operations against enemy shipping —especially U-boats. In World War I it was used for seaplanes; in the second as an RAF fighter station, an air-sea rescue station and an anti-U-boat campaign centre.

75 The 'Fencibles' by Alexander Gibson. Drilling at the Garrison in about 1870. This locally raised force was three-hundred strong at the time of the Napoleonic Wars: a wet plate stereo.

76   German merchant ships, by John Gibson. These vessels are taking shelter in the Roadstead at the outbreak of the Franco-Prussian War, 1870.

77   Seaplane on Town Beach, by Herbert Gibson. Tresco was a seaplane base during World War I.

78 French refugees coming in to Town Quay, by James Gibson.

When the German Army overran France in 1940 many French people escaped to Britain by sea; these eight men—here being interviewed by a Customs officer, who boarded their craft in the Roadstead—arrived at St Mary's in May 1940.

79 Sunderland flying boat by James Gibson.

This RAF aeroplane of World War II is on Town Beach beside the blacksmith's shop, waiting for repairs to a float.

80 Tank landing craft by James Gibson. These vessels took shelter in Scilly during bad weather and were conveniently beached on St Mary's.

SEA BIRDS

Scilly with its many, varied and, in many cases rare, breeds attracts bird-watchers from all over Britain.

Alexander Gibson, in his guide book, was at some pains to claim that his photographs of the wild birds of Scilly were 'a remarkable collection which no visitor should miss seeing'. His descendants, who are duly respectful of other aspects of his work, are less enthusiastic about this.

Certainly he had considerable physical problems; while Frank, with a lightweight, single-lens reflex and follow focus telephoto lens, has many advantages his grandfather did not possess. Alexander, loaded with a heavy camera and tripod, could hardly have hoped to jump ashore from a heaving small boat on to such steep and craggy rocks as Men-a-Vaur, Mincarlo, Illswilgig and Castle Bryher, and scramble over boulders and up rock faces to the birds' nesting grounds. He was limited then by having to use a tripod and focusing on pre-selected spots, because once the plate was in position no re-focusing was possible. His grandson, of course, has complete control over focus to the moment the shutter is fired.

Modern equipment gives the bird photographer so many advantages; in addition the birds and bird-watching are so much better understood than they were that, while in other sections the whole family contributes, Frank's file on sea birds—from which these are a small selection—is authoritative.

His work in this respect is not solely a matter of photography; he has studied and understood sea birds; otherwise he could never have achieved these photographs.

81 Puffin, by Frank Gibson.

The puffin, with its large red and yellow striped beak, is the entertainer among the sea birds of Scilly. It nests in the islands between April and July.

82   Ring Plover, by Frank Gibson.
A native of Scilly, the ring plover, with its smart black collar and clear white breast, is constantly to be seen along the beaches.

83   Fulmar in flight by Frank Gibson.
Like the martlets of mythology, fulmars cannot stand up; they are found round the more lonely rocks like Hanjague.

84   Manx Shearwater
       by Frank Gibson.
These birds, of the petrel species, are ocean creatures, nesting in burrows and usually only coming out by night. Many of them nest on Annet.

85　Roseate Tern,
　　　by Frank Gibson.

Terns come to Scilly during the
summer months. The roseate
tern, with longer tail streamers
than the common tern, is a rare
bird, but is sometimes to be seen
on Stony Island off Samson.

86　Stormy Petrel
　　　by Frank Gibson.

Very rarely seen in Britain, the
stormy petrel, extremely small
for a sea bird, generally lives far
out to sea. They breed on Annet
in Scilly but only leave their
nests by night.

87　Guillemot　hatching　its
　　　young by Frank Gibson.

The chick emerging from the
shell: a skilful, patient, well-
timed piece of photography.

ROUND THE ISLANDS

There is both unity and variety within Scilly: it is possible—but can be dangerous—to generalise about the islands.

The climate is at worst mild; in summer, warm; for the rest, the weather varies between gale, the usual breeze and the utter stillness of fog. The wind is often so keen that sea-facing windows on Porthcressa have been sand-blasted near to opacity. The islands are of granite; their characteristics are rocks, sand, gorse, lichen, the ice plant *mesembryanthemum*, and pink sea thrift. All the islands show pronounced differences between their battered weather sides and the gentler, sheltered parts. It has been suggested that, in prehistory, Scilly was a sacred burial place, and may have been the 'place of the dead' of Celtic legend. Certainly there are vastly more Bronze Age tombs on the islands than in any comparable area of England.

Scilly's glory is its light. Except in fog, the air is so clear that every feature in sight is startlingly sharper than in the heavier atmosphere of the mainland. Everything looks so much closer that the newcomer must make conscious adjustment. The sea, too, is clearer and bluer—blue as the Mediterranean; there is not the algae or general pollution that make the seas of the English coast greenly opaque; and round most of the islands the sea bottom can be seen as clearly as if through glass. Generally, too, the water level between the islands is shallow; it is said that, if the seabed were four or five fathoms higher, all but Western Scilly might be a single island. Alexander Gibson wrote of 'a company of men' walking from Innisidgen to St Martin's and on to Tresco and Bryher in a single low tide.

When the sun is high, the view from Carn Morval Point west and north-west to Samson, Bryher, Tresco and the host of rocks about them is a glittering splendour of sea, land and sky. The sunsets—the Victorians used to promenade on the Garrison to appreciate them fully—are quite spectacular.

The reference books say there are a hundred and forty islands in Scilly; only forty are more than small groups of rocks; and six of them—St Mary's, Tresco, Bryher, St Martins, St Agnes and—if admitted separately—the Gugh —are inhabited. Of the others, Samson, Tean, St Helens' and, briefly, Rosevear, were occupied in relatively recent times. The population has lately grown back to two thousand, four-fifths of whom live on St Mary's. This is the same total figure as in 1901, though still substantially—nearly four hundred—less than that of 1810.

Architecturally Scilly is undistinguished. Domestic housing on St Mary's is of two kinds: the pre-1950, in local stone, consists mostly of unpretentious granite cottages; more recent developments, including flats, are of materials imported as inexpensively as possible from England—they might be anywhere.

The off islands tend to suffer from the fact that builders' goods—like anything else from the mainland—must carry two, if not three, sets of freight charges; and the consequent economies, especially on farm sheds, shelters or lean-tos can be obtrusive.

The population is restricted by comparative inaccessibility—it is 42 miles from Penzance to St Mary's by sea—limitations of water supply, strict control of building, and the conscientiously preservationist attitude of the

Duchy of Cornwall. The notoriously rough sea-crossing—no vessel of greater draught than the ten feet of the present packet could come into the quay at St Mary's at ordinary low water—discourages all but the hardier day-trippers from a second visit. The limited available accommodation, the ban on caravans and dormobiles, and close control over camping, keeps the number of holidaymakers within assimilable limits. As a holiday centre Scilly is simply itself: a place of sun, sea, flowers, sea birds and prehistoric remains, with four pubs and one cinema, where the daily tempo is unhurried, noise is slight; and the motor car is not allowed to dominate life; but it has none of the popular attractions of the usual modern resort.

For an island of only sixteen hundred acres, two miles long by two at its broadest (often narrower—yet nearly ten miles round) St Mary's offers a remarkable—and often overlooked—number of facets and depths. Surprising as it may seem to visitors, the 'country people' of St Mary's *do* come to town in Hugh Town; and Hugh Town people *do* go out into the country. There is a difference of character between the people and, even more positively, between the two settings—as was until quite recently apparent in another small island, Alderney.

Dominated by the Garrison hill and its best building—the sixteenth-century fort, now an hotel, called Star Castle—Hugh Town is like a Cornish village, with shops among nineteenth-century houses, plus some administrative buildings of more than village stature. It is seen in its happiest perspective and balance from Samson. Old Town, the 'capital' of the island until it was superseded by the military importance of Hugh Town, set in a dip with an ancient church and many graves of shipwreck victims, is a slightly forlorn village, attractive in parts though not over-well preserved. Bronze Age graves, a Roman village, gentle rural country, sea-worked rocks, flower farms, minute islands, savage headlands, generous bays and the unending traffic of the harbour make for an island of diverting variety.

St Agnes, chief of the Western Isles, bare, gorse-covered, stone-dotted, and long the pilots' base, is—especially at its southern end—a place of hostile sea-rocks in cruel, deep-water currents, and of many shipwrecks. It has the oldest lighthouse but one in Britain; disused since 1911, it is now a private house, but is still painted white by Trinity House to serve as a daymark. The sixty or so people of its closely linked community, who themselves built the concrete road across the island, are divided by rolling country between Lower Town, Middle Town and Higher Town. The small, old port of Periglis is all but deserted. It is said that St Agnes is not, strictly speaking, entitled to sainthood and it is now generally called simply 'Agnes'. A sandbar—submerged at high tide—connects it to the Gugh with its farm, many ancient graves and a nine-foot stone known as 'The Old Man of Gugh'.

Further to the west, Annet of the five rock-teeth is a bird sanctuary: shearwaters, puffins and tern breed there—and rabbits. Still further out, the Western Rocks include Rosevear where the men who built the Bishop light were housed; and brine-drenched Gorregan, an old hiding place for contraband. The Bishop itself is the furthest west of all, warning shipping against the Western Rocks.

The rounded, two-hill island of Samson is now once more uninhabited; its last few cottages crumbling. It was once Augustus Smith's deer park; now it is occupied only by the breed of black rabbits he introduced.

Bryher, of the five hills, is a peaceful enough place on its eastern—or Tresco—side, where The Town stands back up from the Quay, and round the almost sentimental Rushy Bay to the south. Watch Hill affords a spectacular view across the islands and, at the northerly end, Shipman Head and Hell Bay are two of the most spectacularly stormy pieces of the coast.

Beyond are the north-western outriders—Gweal, Scilly Rock, Castle Bryher, Illiswilgig, Seal Rock, Maiden Bower and Mincarlo.

Tresco, the most sheltered of the islands—in its southern half, the clear wind which characterises the others is not so apparent—is also in some ways the most sophisticated; and, largely by contrivance, has the most varied terrain. It is the home of the Dorrien-Smith family, with the tropical gardens created by Augustus Smith, his Victorian-Gothic Abbey House, his Valhalla; King Charles's Castle, Cromwell's Castle and the cave called Piper's Hole. No cars—only pony trap or tractor—no dogs; the visitor must pay to land and to visit the 'Valhalla'. Northwethal, bleak, bare and dotted with barrows lies between Tresco and St Helens.

St Helens, an unfriendly, stony, steep, small island, no longer inhabited, has the remains of the oldest church in Scilly, a small walled harbour and the ruins of the pest house which was an eighteenth-century quarantine station for infected ships. Appropriately it is a home of the savage greater black-backed gull. A little to the north is Round Island with its red-flashing light.

In the seventeenth century, the first of the Nance family to come to Scilly arrived from Falmouth to start the kelp industry on Tean—pronounced 'Te-an'. Stonily bare, with a central hill, it still has the ruins of a granite cottage, old kelp kilns and many prehistoric graves.

The towns—Lower, Middle and Higher—and most of the flower farms of St Martin's lie to the south west; the bare, high downland, angry rocks, howling winds, cliffs and gulls, to the north east. The striking—and misdated—red-and-white Daymark is on St Martin's Head, at its eastern tip; and White Island lies to the north.

The Eastern Isles, of sandbars, wiry grass, heather, brambles, sea thrift, birds and seals are less unfriendly than the Western Rocks. Hanjague is their most hostile member. Great Arthur (reputedly haunted and formerly used by smugglers as a cache), Great Ganilly and—much earlier—Nornour (where a prehistoric village has recently been excavated) were inhabited; now the group—of about a dozen—are the territory of boat trippers, bird-watchers, crab and lobster fishermen. There, behind them, is Innisidgen, with all the north-east side of St Mary's; the circle is complete.

These hundred-and-forty granite islands have stood up against the Western Ocean for at least four thousand years: they were inhabited before 1000 BC. The Gibson family camera has turned an observant and understanding eye on the last century of that life.

88 'The Bank' by Alexander Gibson. Taken from the front of the present chemist's shop, looking down Hugh Street. A nostalgic composition, probably of 1870 or even earlier; noticeably before the tourist trade had turned the houses into holiday accommodation or shops.

89 Star Castle by John Gibson. Catching all the granite starkness of the original fortress, before it was converted into a hotel: from a wet plate.

90   Hugh Town School by Alexander Gibson. Taken c 1890-1900: after the restoration of the church but before the Methodist chapel was built. All but the little girl with her back to the camera and the woman peeping from the upstairs window have been 'organised'.

91   The carpet cart by Herbert Gibson. This 'gipsy' used to pay a hard-working but profitable annual visit to St Mary's selling carpets, linoleum and wicker chairs. His customers from the off islands came by boat to buy.

92　*Bonnet* by Frank Gibson. One of the pilot gigs on Town Beach, St Mary's. These six-oared boats—believed now to be almost unique to Scilly—are nowadays used solely for races which take place on Friday evenings during the finer half of the year. The usual distance is about a mile from Nut Rock, east of Samson, to the point of St Mary's Quay; but other courses are sometimes used. Of the six gigs based on islands, three—*Bonnet*, *Golden Eagle* and *Nornour*—represent St Mary's; *Czar*, Tresco and Bryher combined; *Dolphin*, St Martin's; and *Shah* St Agnes. Occasionally, at the end of the season, a crew from Newquay—the only available competitors—bring their gig on the steamer and join in the competition, which ends extremely convivially.

93　Hugh Town and Harbour by Frank Gibson.
Taken from the golf course in light typical of spring in Scilly, Taylor's Island in the foreground and Newford Island beyond—a photograph that shows how precariously low Hugh Town lies on its narrow sand strip between the granite hills.

The sea has more than once met across it.

94 Hugh Town under snow by Alexander Gibson. Snow is almost unknown on Scilly. This was taken from Sally Port after the great blizzard of 1891. Who was pressed into service to provide a visual break in the foreground by trudging ankle-deep across the snow?

95   Buzza Tower by Alexander Gibson.
An untouched photograph of the tower as it was
in 1900.

96   Buzza Tower by Alexander Gibson.
A 'reconstruction' taken in about 1880: the sails,
which had not existed since much earlier, were
painted in by Alexander.

97 The House with the Plant in the Garden by Herbert Gibson. Clarence House, Church Street, where the Gibson family lived and which was later converted to include the shop.

98 The Shop by Frank Gibson. James Gibson built this shop out across the garden of Clarence House in 1937.

99 A House in Blood Alley, Hugh Town, by Alexander Gibson.

A surprising—uncommissioned and unpaid—domestic view of Hugh Town as late as 1898. Blood Alley has now disappeared; it ran between the Park and the Strand and consisted largely of former coastguard cottages. Alexander, sensing his picture, called Mrs Barrett out from her cooking; the two girls are her daughters; the boy, Clem Guy, later emigrated to Australia. The door on the left led to 'Johnny Pat's' crab-pot store.

100 Well Lane by Alexander Gibson.

An almost painfully posed, yet revealing, street scene of the 1890s, celebrating the renovation and decoration of some Hugh Town houses (compare this with plate 99—Blood Alley—of roughly the same date). Well Place is through the present Post Office arch.

101 Hugh Town Church by John Gibson.
An early photograph, of about 1870; shipbuilding was still in progress on Town Beach:
planks for the purpose—cut at the sawmill which
then stood beside the camera—are stacked on the
left.

102 The Old Custom House by Alexander
Gibson.

About 1880: the Customs officer is standing in the
doorway. The building is now the Atlantic Hotel.

103   The Atlantic Hotel by James Gibson. As late as 1935. The hotel porter is Bill Perrin.

104   Hugh Town by Alexander Gibson. Taken from Carn Thomas in 1890: Buzza Hill and Tower in the distance; the Strand and Town Beach below.

105 Hugh Town by Frank Gibson.
Taken from above Porth Mellon in 1970, this catches the clear-aired brightness of Scilly.

106 Smuggler's stone by Alexander Gibson.
An item from the Gibson museum; the groove cut in the stone took the rope by which contraband, which had to be concealed, was sunk and anchored.

107 Anchors, Hugh Town by Alexander Gibson.
A study stylistically ahead of its time in 1900.

108 Artifacts by Alexander Gibson.
More items from the family museum since passed
to the official establishment: tinder box, flint and
steel, candle, plaited straw, fish-oil lamp.

109 Preparing for sailing by Frank Gibson. A modern summer scene on Town Beach.

110 St Mary's Quay by Alexander Gibson. A day-trip by sailing boat; pinnace and fishing vessels. The sailing party were visiting geology students. (See also plates 126 and 127).

111 At St Mary's Airport by Frank Gibson.
On this day in 1964 the Scilly air service was changed from 'Rapide' aeroplanes to helicopters.

112 Burial Chamber, Normandy Downs by Alexander Gibson.
This well-known—and, so far as archaeologists are concerned, too well worn—chamber is one of a number on the west of St Mary's. The figure in the chamber resembles Alexander and it is assumed that he focussed the camera, took up position, and made the exposure by some form of remote control or assistance.

113   Holy Vale by Alexander Gibson. Holy Vale Farm, the home of the Mumford family, one of the
first to join the flower industry.

114 Carn Leh by Frank Gibson.
This weathered stone, standing near Old Town, was one of the earlier tourist sights of St Mary's.

115 Sir Clowdisley Shovell's grave by Alexander Gibson.

A reconstruction, made before the erection of the memorial stone. The Admiral's body—and the stern name-board of his flagship, *Association*—were washed ashore at this point in Porth Hellick Bay where he was first buried by islanders and subsequently removed and reinterred in Westminster Abbey. The rock-formation in the distance is 'The Loaded Camel'.

116   Old Town Church by Alexander Gibson. Like plate 94, taken after the blizzard of 1891. This
         building was formerly the nave of a larger, cruciform church.

117   Old Town by Alexander Gibson. This can be dated as about 1884. All the houses except the first
         on the left are now gone and have been replaced by the new estate.

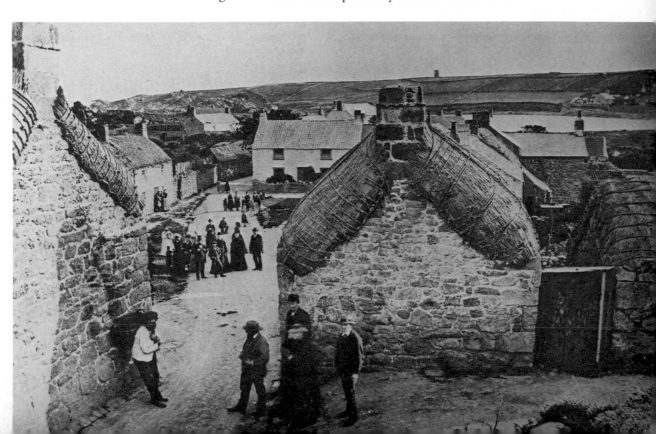

118   Old Town by Alexander Gibson. Looking towards the Quay; taken in the 1880s.

119 Nag's Head, St Agnes by Frank Gibson. A typically agonised rock formation of the islands. The original lighthouse—of 1680—is beyond.

120 The Bar by Frank Gibson. This sand bar, dangerous when covered by a high tide, connects Agnes with the Gugh.

121 The Wishing Well, St Agnes by Alexander Gibson. This was a popular postcard of one of the
earlier tourist attractions; the well can still be seen.

122 Bishop Rock Lighthouse by Herbert Gibson.
The workmen are carrying out the third major
constructional operation on the Bishop Light.
The first—an open, cast-iron structure—was
washed away in 1850 before it was used. Its
successor, built in stone, was damaged in a storm
and judged to be insecure in heavy seas; so the
final operation was the recasing of 1887. These
men are putting on that outer, reinforcing 'skin';
they also added another two storeys to raise it to
its present height.

123   Inside the Bishop Light by James Gibson.
The lighthouse-keeper's room, with commemora-
tive plaques: taken during the 1930s.

124 On Rosevear by Herbert Gibson.

The final choice of the site for the western light on Scilly was made between the Bishop Rock and Rosevear, two miles to the south east. When the Bishop was selected, most of the lighthouse builders were housed on Rosevear, a small, barren, stony rock, barely above spring tide level. A blacksmith's shop was constructed, as well as living accommodation. They even contrived to play games; and it is said that they once held a dance there with partners imported from St Agnes. When Herbert went to the island in the 1890s this was the most substantial building remaining. There could hardly be a finer example of the non-commercial enthusiasm of the Gibson photographers in making a pictorial record of the history of Scilly.

125 Round Island light by Alexander Gibson.

An engaging period piece, taken in the 1890s at a time when a visit to Round Island lighthouse was a Scillonian occasion. Surprisingly enough to the modern mind, these long-frocked ladies made the journey from St Mary's—Tresco, Bryher or St Martin's—to Round Island by small sailing boat or even rowing boat, negotiated the extremely awkward landing and yet contrived to make their promenade as elegantly as this. Visits to the island were banned after a visitor fell and sued Trinity House for compensation.

126 'Armorel's Cottage' by Alexander Gibson. This cottage on Samson was the setting for the sentimental Victorian novel *Armorel of Lyonesse* (1890)—a best seller in its day—by Sir Walter Besant. That success prompted this photo of the ruin which still retained the tamarisk, on the left, and the elder, on the right, of the novelist's description.

127 'Armorel's Cottage' by Alexander Gibson. This view of the cottage, taken on the same trip as the previous plate—in the 1890s—shows John Gibson sitting in the foreground, Herbert Gibson reclining on top of the wall, and, below, the group of geological students of plate 110.

128   Kist on Samson by Alexander Gibson. This kist was in a barrow opened by Augustus Smith in 1863 which contained burnt remains.

129   Bryher by Frank Gibson. Looking down towards the church and harbour; showing the floral hedges about the flower 'squares'.

130   Bryher Church by Alexander Gibson. The balance of this photograph is a matter of sensibility; its clarity could not have been achieved with late nineteenth-century equipment except in the sparkingly clear atmosphere of Scilly.

131 Tresco by Alexander Gibson. Half the houses in the right middle have gone; others were incorporated into the hotel. The 'Man o' War' rock lies in the middle distance.

132 Tresco by Alexander Gibson. An impressively high-quality early photograph, taken in 1887 before the lighthouse on Round Island was built.

133   Tresco by James Gibson.
An aerial photograph showing the Abbey Pool in
the foreground; the 'Abbey' between it and the
Great Pool; gardens to its left; New Grimsby on
the sea edge, and the tip of Tresco beyond.

134   Tropical Gardens, Tresco by James Gibson.
Tropical and sub-tropical plants collected by
Augustus Smith, and others brought back for him
by sailors from Scilly, were planted in the Lord
Proprietor's garden. Though they would not
have grown anywhere else in Britain, they
flourished in the protected, almost humid,
atmosphere enjoyed in Scilly only by the southern
half of this one island.

135 Cromwell's Castle, Tresco by James Gibson. After the third and final surrender of Royalists to Parliamentary forces in Scilly, this fort was built on Tresco. In many circumstances it could afford more valuable harbourage to a fleet of that period than St Mary's.

136 Houses on Tresco by Alexander Gibson. Described by Alexander as 'Smuggler's Cottages' this row, then—in the 1880s—at Old Grimsby, near what is now the Island Hotel, has entirely disappeared. Notice the communal water barrel and the washing—and the fish—drying in the sun.

137 Houses on Tresco by Alexander Gibson. A slightly later photograph of the houses in the previous plate, taken from the opposite end of the row.

138 Mill on Tresco by Alexander Gibson.
Alexander Gibson described this as a cider press or 'tin crusher', but it bears a strong resemblance to the kind of corn mill which was worked by a horse—or a man—turning a rotary arm to power the grinding stone.

139 Piper's Hole, Tresco by Herbert Gibson.
The two men sitting at the bottom are John Gibson on the right, Alexander on the left. They are in the entrance to this initially unimpressive, but subsequently interesting, cave.

140 The 'Valhalla', Tresco by Frank Gibson
The 'Valhalla'—an admission charge is made
—is an exhibition of happily recovered and
cleverly refurbished figureheads of ships wrecked
on the rocks of Scilly.

141 The Pest House, St Helens by Alexander
Gibson.
An ordinance of 1757 established St Helens Pool
as the quarantine station for ships north of
Finisterre with plague or similar infection aboard.

142   On St Martin's by Alexander Gibson. Building the original 'old' quay at St Martin's.

143   Men at St Martin's by Alexander Gibson. These are the workmen who built the 'new'—or 'Par'—quay after the 'old' Quay was destroyed by a storm. Every one of them was a St Martin's man.

144   St Martin's by Frank Gibson. View towards Higher Town; granite walls giving way to hedges
to protect the 'squares'.

145　St Martin's School by Alexander Gibson.
The building still exists actively as a school and has been extended. The former schoolmaster for almost fifty years—a friend of the Gibsons by the name of Culyer—used to have *The Times* sent to him and, when he considered its contents sufficiently important, he would sit outside the school door and read them to the islanders.

146　Kelping by Alexander Gibson.
'Old Ford' gathering seaweed on St Martin's in the way it was collected for kelping, and later for fertilising.

147 *Mesembryanthemum* by Frank Gibson.
The ice plant; one of the characteristic flowers
of Scilly.

148   A field in Scilly by Frank Gibson.
Pink sea thrift—or sea pinks—in bloom; the other
characteristic 'wild' flower of the islands.

150 Tooth Rock, Peninnis by Frank Gibson.
In the Isles of Scilly that for four thousand years
have stood up against the Western Ocean.

149 The *Scillonian* by Frank Gibson.
Taken from Carn Morval, St Mary's: the service
boat is heading down the Roadstead towards
Crow Sound on the return journey to Penzance;
Tresco and Bryher are beyond.

BIBLIOGRAPHY

Borlase, William *Observations on the ancient and present state of the Islands of Scilly* (1756).

Bowley, R. L. *The Fortunate Islands: A History of Scilly* (1945).

Bowley, R. L. *The Isles of Scilly* (31st edition 1971/72).

Cameron, Julia Margaret *Victorian Photographs* (1926).

Gibson, A. & H. *The Isles of Scilly: the Visitor's Companion in Sunny Lyonnesse* (1925).

Gibson, F. E. *The Isles of Scilly* (nd).

Gibson, F. E. *Pictorial Guide to the Seabirds of the Isles of Scilly* (1969).

Grigson, Geoffrey *The Scilly Isles* (1948).

Heath, Robert *A Natural and Historical Account of the Isles of Scilly* (1750).

Larn, Richard *Cornish Shipwrecks: Volume 3—The Isles of Scilly* (1971).

Leland, John *Itinerary* (1710).

Mumford, Clive *Portrait of the Isles of Scilly* (1967).

Woodley, George *A View of the Present State of the Islands of Scilly* (1822).

The Scillonian (Quarterly, 1925 to date).